D1418477

MEASURING UP
length

Peter Patilla

New Discovery Books
New York

First published in Great Britain in 1999 by
Belitha Press Limited,
London House, Great Eastern Wharf,
Parkgate Road, London SW11 4NQ

Series editor: Claire Edwards
Editor: Russell Mclean
Series designer: Simeen Karim
Designer: Double Elephant/Rita Wüthrich
Picture researcher: Juliet Duff
Consultant: Martin Hollins

Thanks to Thomas and Joseph Shipman for being the readers; Graham Peacock
of Sheffield Hallam University and Ken Rickwood of Essex University for clarifying
some science ideas; and Alison Patilla for research.

Published in the United States by
New Discovery Books
An Imprint of Macmillan Library Reference USA
1633 Broadway, New York, NY 10019

Printed in Singapore   10 9 8 7 6 5 4 3 2 1

Library of Congress Cataloging-in-Publication Data
Patilla, Peter.
      Length / by Peter Patilla : [illustrator, Dave Cockcroft].
         p.   cm. -- (Measuring up)
      Includes index.
      Summary: Discusses the origins of our present-day measuring systems, how people
measured lengths in the past, the different systems and how to convert from one to
another, and examples of unusual lengths.
      ISBN 0-382-42233-3
      1. Mensuration--Juvenile literature.   [1. Measurement.]   I. Cockcroft, David, ill.
II. Title.   III. Series.
QA465.P34   1999
530.8--dc21   98-49372
                                                                              CIP
                                                                              AC

Picture acknowledgments:
Ancient Art and Architecture: 12; **Biro Bic Ltd**: 28; **Bridgeman Art Library**: 5 Giraudon,
8 Victoria & Albert Museum, London, 11 British Library, London, 17 left Giraudon, 18 Index;
Corbis: 9 Yann Arthus-Bertrand; **Eye Ubiquitous**: 29; **Michael Holford**: 10; **Ordnance Survey**:
27 © Crown Copyright License Number MC 88667M0001; **Photodisc**: front cover; **Science and
Society Photo Library**: 7b, 13, 15; **Science Photo Library**: 17r Jean-Loup Charmet, 23 left
Dr. Mitsuo Ohtsuki, 25t Philippe Plailly; **Tony Stone Images**: 7t, 20, 22, 23r, 25b, 26.

CONTENTS

IN THE BEGINNING

All through history, people have found it necessary to measure how long things are. The earliest ways of measuring length were quite simple—people used parts of the body, such as palms, hands, and feet, as units of length.

palm

One of the most popular body units was the cubit. This was measured as the distance from the elbow to the tip of the outstretched middle finger. Early builders in Egypt and Babylon used the cubit as one of their main units of length. The length of a cubit varied from place to place, but, on average, it equaled about 20 inches.

cubit

Palms

A palm was the width of f[our] closed fingers, not includi[ng] the thumb. Hands (4 inch[es]) are still used to measure [the] height of a horse. A han[d] is also used to measure bananas. A small bunch is a hand, a large bunc[h] is a stem. A span is th[e] distance from the tip [of] the little finger to the tip [of] the thumb when the fingers are spread out.

span

Fingers

The unit of a digit or finger was used when measuring small objects. A digit measurement is the width of the forefinger across the first joint.

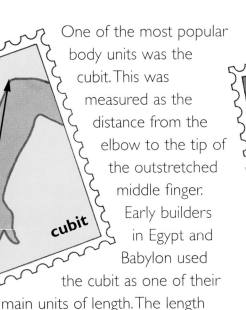

digit

Feet

At first, a foot was the distance from the heel to the toe. A pace or stride was a measure of longer distances. People paced out a distance, trying to keep each pace the same size.

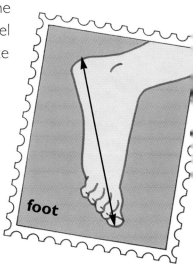

foot

In the Bible, Noah was told to build an ark that was 300 cubits long, 50 cubits wide, and 30 cubits tall.

Did you know?
The deepest part of the Pacific Ocean is the Marianas Trench. It is about 6,000 fathoms (36,000 feet) deep. If you dropped a metal ball from a boat, it would take more than an hour to reach the ocean floor.

Fathoms

The distance from fingertip to fingertip with arms outstretched is called a fathom. This unit was used by sailors to measure the depth of water. They would lower a weighted rope over the side of the boat and count how many fathoms of rope they used before it hit the bottom. The name comes from an old English word, *faethmian*, which means to use both arms. Fathoms are still used sometimes to measure depths under the ocean.

Length fact
When the navigator of a paddle steamer sounds a depth of 1 fathom, he shouts "Mark one." At 2 fathoms, he cries "Mark twain." Author Samuel Clemens was so fond of these boats that he changed his name to Mark Twain. One of his best-known books is *The Adventures of Huckleberry Finn*.

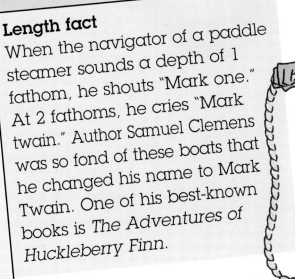

EARLY STANDARD UNITS

The problem with using body parts as measures of length is that people are different sizes— so these units were never very accurate.

Over the years, people tried to sort out the confusion over different-sized body lengths. They began to agree on the length of certain units. These standard units made measuring more accurate for people who lived, worked, and traded together. Among the first people to develop accurate units were the Egyptians. Their standards date back to about 3000 B.C.

Length fact
Egyptian children learned that:

1 cubit	=	7 palms
1 small cubit	=	6 palms
1 small span	=	3 palms
1 large span	=	3½ palms
1 palm	=	4 digits
1 hand	=	5 digits

Royal cubits

These Egyptian units were based on the digit, palm, span, and cubit. A standard royal master cubit was first made from black granite. This was 7 palms long and divided into 28 main sections, each of 1 digit. Some of these digit sections were divided up further. These little divisions meant that for the first time people could measure lengths very accurately. Then, all the cubit sticks used throughout Egypt had to be matched against the master cubit.

Babylonian cubits

About 4,000 years ago, the Babylonians also used the cubit, sometimes called a *kus*, as a unit of length. The Babylonian cubit was also divided into smaller units, each called a *shusi*. There were 30 shusi in a cubit.

Chinese lengths

Parts of the body were used as measuring units in ancient China, too. The distance from the pulse in the wrist to the base of the thumb was used for short lengths. Units with the same name varied in length from region to region, and for different uses. Stonemasons and carpenters all had their own sizes of units.

The chih and the chang

In 221 B.C., Emperor Shi Huangdi ordered that two basic measures called the chih and the chang should be used as standard units. In today's measurements, the chih would be about 10 inches long and the chang about 12 feet long. Like most Chinese units, these were then divided into ten smaller sections.

The Egyptians made beautiful and very accurate tools for measuring length, such as this stone cubit stick.

Egyptian builders working on the pyramids at Giza used cubit sticks to work out measurements with extraordinary precision. The four sides of the Great Pyramid are accurate to within a few centimeters of each other, even though they are more than 750 feet long.

Did you know?
The oldest standard unit of length dates from about 2100 B.C. It was based on the statue of the ruler Gudea of Lagash (in modern-day Iraq). The foot of the statue is about 10 inches long and is divided into 16 parts.

INVADERS AND TRADERS

As a result of invasions and the spread of trade,
the Greeks, and then the Romans, influenced
how length was measured throughout Europe.

The Greeks and the Romans spread across
Europe, Africa, and western Asia between
about 1000 B.C. and A.D. 400. Wherever they
went, they used their own units of length,
which became the basis for local systems in
different parts of the world. The main Greek
lengths were the finger, the foot, and the
Olympic cubit. There were 16 fingers in a
foot and 24 fingers in a cubit. The Roman
units included the foot, the pace, and the rod.

Charlemagne's foot

The Roman units of length were still used
throughout Europe in the Middle Ages. But
these units had changed over time and from
country to country. In A.D. 789 the Emperor
of Europe, Charlemagne, ordered everyone
to use the royal foot (the length of his own
foot) as the standard length. But despite
his efforts, most people kept on using
the units they were used to.

Trading standards

During the Middle Ages, people traveled
across Europe to buy and sell goods at huge
trade fairs. To avoid cheating, every trader had
to use standard units of length. The ell was a
very important unit, because it was used to
measure cloth, a valuable item at that time.
In some countries, an ell was the distance
between two elbows with arms outstretched.
In Holland, it was the distance between bent
elbows with the hands clenched and touching
the chest. To clear up the confusion, at trade
fairs in the Champagne region of France,
every ell stick was checked against a standard
iron bar about 30 inches long.

The Emperor Charlemagne (A.D. *742–814*)

Traders at the Champagne fairs had to check their lengths of cloth against the iron standard held by the Keeper of the Fair.

Explorers to America

In the 1500s, Europeans sailed to America and began to settle there. They brought their own systems of measurement, which spread to the American colonies, too. Modern American measures, called U.S. customary units, are based on these early European units of length.

Did you know?
One of the oldest units of length was called a stadium. It was the length of the original racetrack at Olympia, in ancient Greece. This was about 670 feet long.

Fingers and nails

Fingers and nails were important measurements in the clothmaking industry. A finger was defined as 4½ inches (about 11 centimeters). Some people measured a nail from the tip of the middle finger to the second knuckle, which was half a finger. Others measured it across the four nails with fingers closed. The hems on cloaks were usually one nail wide—about 2¼ inches.

The site of the racetrack at Olympia, in Greece.

MEASURING THE LAND

It was important for farmers to know exactly how much land they owned. Most of the units they invented are no longer used, but the names remain in our language even today.

Did you know?
The chain is no longer used—except in England on the cricket pitch. The length of the wicket is exactly 1 chain (22 yards).

The Egyptians were among the first people to use chains and knotted ropes to measure their land. Every year the Nile River would flood and wash away markers at the edges of the fields. After the flood, farmers needed to measure out the land again as accurately as possible. Later, in about 300 B.C., the Greeks used knotted floating lines to measure their coastline.

Gunter's chain

In the seventeenth century an English mathematician called Edmund Gunter devised a special chain made up of 100 links. This was exactly 22 yards long. Gunter's chain was such an accurate instrument for measuring land that it was used by farmers and surveyors until the middle of the twentieth century.

This Egyptian painting on the wall of a tomb shows farmers measuring a field of corn with a knotted rope.

Rods

Rods were one of the earliest and most important standard units of length for measuring land. Later, they also came to be known as poles or perches. There were originally ten Roman feet in a rod. Over time, the rod grew to a length of 5½ yards (5 meters). In the Middle Ages, a rod was worked out by lining up 16 men outside church on a Sunday morning and measuring the total length of their left feet. From the sixteenth century onwards, there were 4 rods in a chain.

Furlongs

A furlong was defined as the distance a team of oxen could plough a furrow before they needed to rest. The name comes from the phrase "furrow long." It measured 220 yards (about 201 meters), so there were exactly 8 furlongs in a mile. During the Middle Ages, furlongs were mainly used to measure around the edge of a field. Today, furlongs are still used to measure horse racetracks.

Leagues

A league was a long unit used by the Greeks in the first centuries A.D. The name *league* was taken from the Ancient Gauls, who lived in Northern Europe from around 400 B.C. An English league equaled 3 miles.

This scene shows oxen ploughing a furrow in about A.D. 1050. By 1500, a furlong was defined as 125 paces.

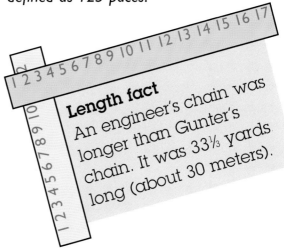

Length fact
An engineer's chain was longer than Gunter's chain. It was 33⅓ yards long (about 30 meters).

FEET AND INCHES

For hundreds of years, the most common units used to measure short distances were feet and inches. These have now been largely replaced by the metric system, but they are still used in the United States and some other parts of the world.

This mosaic was made in about the fourth century A.D. *It shows the spirit of creation, called Ktisis, holding a Roman foot ruler.*

An emperor's standard

To make sure that a foot was always the same length, the Romans made copper bars to be used as standard units. The length of the bars probably matched the foot size of a Roman emperor. Each bar was divided into twelve equal parts. The Roman word for a twelfth was *uncia*. This gave us the English word *inch*.

Both the Greeks and the Romans used the foot as a unit of length. People had been using their feet as a rough measuring unit for thousands of years, but a widely-used standard unit was not made until Greek times. The feet and inches used in modern times are based on a system introduced by the Romans, whose standard foot was shorter than the Greek foot. The Romans were the first people to divide the foot into 12 smaller units of equal length.

Length fact
The word *ounce* also comes from the Roman *uncia*. This is because Roman copper foot bars weighed 1 pound. In earlier times there were 12 ounces in a pound.

The line at the bottom of this marble tablet is a Roman or Greek foot measure. The tablet was made in about A.D. 300.

Confusion rules

During the Middle Ages, Roman feet and inches were not used everywhere in Europe. In about 1150, King David I of Scotland defined the inch as the distance across a man's thumb at the base of the nail. But almost 200 years later, King Edward II of England decided that, "the length of an inch shall be equal to three grains of barley, dry and round, placed end to end lengthwise." So throughout the Middle Ages, you could never be sure of the exact length of feet or inches from one country to the next.

U.S. and British inches

Until 1959, the length of a British and an American inch was fractionally different. The U.S. inch equaled 25.40005 millimeters, while the British inch was slightly shorter, equal to 25.39998 millimeters. Although the difference between the two inches was very small, it made things very difficult for aircraft engineers who discovered that American nuts did not quite fit British bolts. After years of confusion, it was finally agreed that a standard inch should be defined as exactly 25.4 millimeters.

MILES AND YARDS

Long distances were often measured in miles and yards. But miles were not always divided into yards—this happened gradually, over centuries.

As centuries passed, people needed to measure long distances more accurately. At first, the mile was divided into 8 furlongs. Eventually, these, in turn, were divided into yards. This slow, haphazard way of dividing explains why there are such an odd number of yards in a mile today.

Length fact
Today there are 3 feet in a yard and 1,760 yards in a mile, although countries have not always agreed about this. The old Swedish mile was 11,500 yards long!

A thousand paces

We have the Romans to thank for the mile as a unit of length. The Roman pace was a double step, about 5 feet (1.5 meters) in length. It was commonly used as a measuring unit. When the Romans marched across conquered lands, they counted out every thousand paces. The Roman phrase for this distance was *mille passus*, from which we get our word *mile*. We can tell from the hundreds of Roman milestones scattered across Europe that the Roman mile was shorter than the one we use today. Romans didn't use yards, but if they had, there would only have been about 1,618 yards in one of their miles.

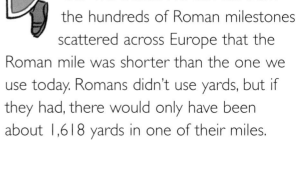

Did you know?
A mile measured at sea
is called a nautical mile,
but different countries do
not agree on its exact length.
In Britain, there are just under
2,027 yards in a nautical
mile. In the U.S., it is only
2,025 yards long.

A royal yardstick

In northern Europe, a yard
was the length of a girdle worn
by the Anglo-Saxons. In European
countries further south, it was a
double cubit, which made it about
1 meter long. Like most measuring units,
yards varied over time and from place to
place. In the 1100s, King Henry I of England
decided that a yard should be the distance
from his nose to the thumb of his outstretched
arm. Because this early yardstick was based
on the arm length of the king, miles, yards,
feet, and inches became known as imperial
measures. In 1215, King John gave orders that
a standard iron yard should measure 3 feet,
each of 12 inches, "neither more nor less."

Measuring in public

Yardsticks were often used as measuring
instruments, but as these became worn
down, they had to be checked regularly
for accuracy. Bronze plaques showing one
yard were displayed in town squares so
that craftworkers and traders could check
the accuracy of their yardsticks.

The Standard Imperial Yard

After centuries of uncertainty over the
length of the yard, it was decided in 1760
that Britain needed one standard measure.
However, the original Standard Imperial Yard
was lost when the Houses of Parliament
were destroyed by fire in 1834. A new
standard, created in 1855, was kept
in a fire-proof lead case, buried in
the walls of the new parliament
building. Every 20 years, the
wall was unbricked and the
standard yard checked
for accuracy.

*This Elizabethan standard
yardstick is made of bronze.
It dates back to around 1582.*

METRIC MEASUREMENTS

The meter is the basic unit of the metric system. The name comes from the Greek word *metron*, which means a measure.

A decimal system of length (one based on the number ten) was first suggested in 1670 by a French vicar, Gabriel Mouton. But his idea was not fully developed until the 1790s, during the French Revolution. The Revolution was a time of enormous change, and the new government demanded a fair measuring system for its people. Scientists wanted a unit that would not change over time or from place to place. So they decided to base the new system not on the human body, but on the dimensions of the earth.

Delambre and Méchain

Scientists declared that the new meter would equal the distance between the North Pole and the equator divided by ten million. But how to measure that distance? The problem was solved by two engineers, Jean Delambre and Pierre Méchain. They decided to measure the distance between Dunkirk, France, and Barcelona, Spain, and then calculate the whole distance from the North Pole to the equator. They did not measure every step of the way, but used their knowledge of geometry to work out distances as they went along. Their journey began in 1792. Seven years later they reached Barcelona, and finally calculated the length of the meter.

Did you know?
Delambre and Méchain were often arrested on suspicion of espionage. People thought they were signaling to enemy forces with their flags and poles!

For all people, for all time

Charles-Maurice de Talleyrand was a clever politician who kept his head through the French Revolution, even though he belonged to an aristocratic family. In 1790, he launched an important debate about weights and measures. The French Academy of Sciences adopted the metric system nine years later, with the motto 'For all people, for all time'.

Charles-Maurice de Talleyrand (1754–1838)

Europe goes metric

After the French Revolution, Napoleon Bonaparte ruled France. He conquered many European countries too, and the metric system slowly spread across Europe due to a Napoleonic decree. Today, most countries use this system for everyday measuring. Some countries, such as Britain, use a mixture of old imperial measurements and newer metric ones. Scientists and engineers all over the world use metric measures.

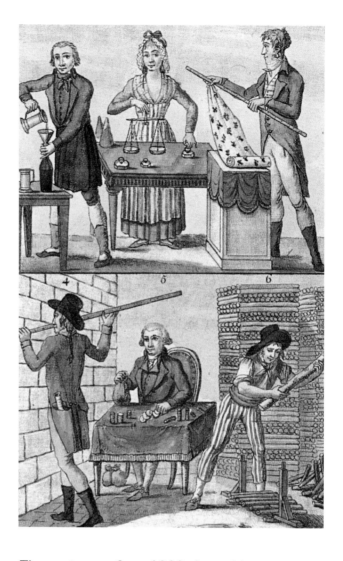

These pictures from 1800 showed how to use the new metric measures introduced during the French Revolution.

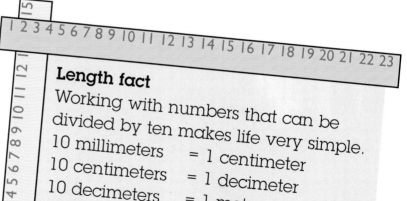

Length fact

Working with numbers that can be divided by ten makes life very simple.

10 millimeters = 1 centimeter
10 centimeters = 1 decimeter
10 decimeters = 1 meter
1000 meters = 1 kilometer

MEASURING INSTRUMENTS

From very early times, people have designed and created special instruments to help them measure more accurately and easily.

The first measuring tools were simple rulers, sticks, and ropes, which have developed into the tools we use today. Egyptian masons used a wooden ruler with a beveled (sloping) edge. Two left-hand palms were pictured on the ruler, each palm divided into digits. Over the years, people have used cubit sticks, rods, yardsticks, and meter sticks to check length. In the Middle Ages, plain rulers with no markings at all were sold. Users probably made their own divisions, depending on what they were measuring. Rulers used in schools today are usually 12 inches or 30 centimeters long.

Fifteenth-century stonemasons (above) used dividers to check the sizes of the stones they built churches with.

Length fact
The most accurate rulers today are called laser interferometers. They are used to calibrate (measure out) the length of rulers, tapes, and other measuring devices.

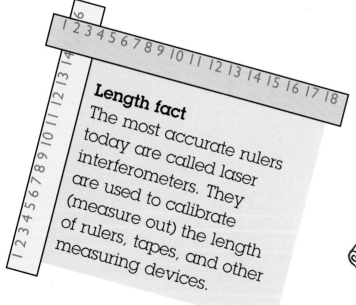

A micrometer (left) is used to measure tiny lengths, like the thickness of paper.

Folding rulers

The Romans invented folding rulers so that people could measure long lengths using an instrument that could be easily carried. They were 6 or 12 inches long and made of bronze. These pocket rulers were used by officials rather than craftworkers, who would have found them too expensive. Folding rulers disappeared with the Romans, and did not reappear until the seventeenth century. The folding rulers we use today are at least a yard or a meter long.

Dividers

It is not known quite when dividers were invented, but they were used by the Greeks and the Romans. Dividers have straight legs with pointed ends, and are used to compare, transfer, or mark-off lengths. For example, if you are planning a walking vacation on a map, you might aim to walk 10 miles every day. Using the map scale, you set the dividers to that distance. Then you can easily mark off equal intervals along your route. Each interval would be one day's walking. Ever since the first maps were drawn up, sailors have used dividers for marking off distances on their charts to help them navigate the oceans.

Calipers

Calipers were invented thousands of years ago. They have curved legs and are used to measure lengths that are difficult to check with a ruler or tape. You can use calipers to measure the length of an egg or a ball. Once the legs are the right distance apart, the the measurement can easily be read from a ruler.

Trundle wheels

Surveyors and others use trundle wheels to measure long distances. Each time the wheel makes one complete revolution, a counter records the distance that it has traveled. Cars have a similar instrument called an odometer that shows the distance of a journey in miles.

LENGTHS AND DIMENSIONS

Length is a measure of how long something is, but we also use units of length in other ways —to describe the size of an object, for example.

The dimensions of an object tell us its size. The words most often used to describe dimensions are *length* (A), *width* or *breadth* (B), and *height* (C). Sometimes these words are confusing. A telephone pole standing upright may be 6 yards tall, but lying on the ground it will be 6 yards long. Width (or breadth) is the measurement of an object from one side to the other. The distance through the middle of an object is its thickness.

Tallness and height

Tallness and height are both vertical measurements. Tallness describes the length of something standing upright, such as a building or a person. Height is the distance of an object from the ground or from sea level. So a girl might be 5 feet tall, but if she climbed a tree she could be 12 feet high. In everyday speech, we often use these words interchangeably.

The world's highest mountain is Mount Everest (left) in the Himalayas, which is 29,028 feet high. The tallest mountain is Mauna Kea, in Hawaii. It is 33,369 feet tall. Most of this is below sea level, leaving only 13,796 feet above the water.

Distance

Distance is how far apart two points are. We talk about the length of a rope, but the distance between two towns. Distance is often measured "as the crow flies," meaning in a straight line. But it is usually impossible to travel between two places in a straight line. Winding roads mean that the journey will be longer than the distance as the crow flies, so it is often more useful to describe the actual distance traveled.

Depth

The word *depth* is used in two ways. The depth of water describes the vertical distance from the surface to the bottom. We might also talk about the depth of a cave. This means how far back the cave stretches, but not how far down it goes.

Perimeter

The length around the edge of an object is called its perimeter. If the object is circular, its perimeter is called the circumference. Hat, collar, and waist sizes are the circumferences of parts of the body. Girth is an old English word meaning the distance around the waist.

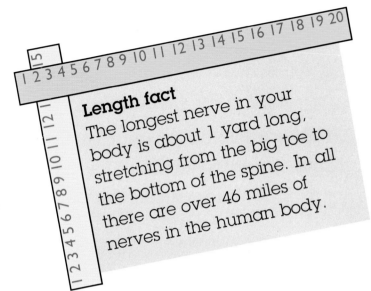

Length fact
The longest nerve in your body is about 1 yard long, stretching from the big toe to the bottom of the spine. In all there are over 46 miles of nerves in the human body.

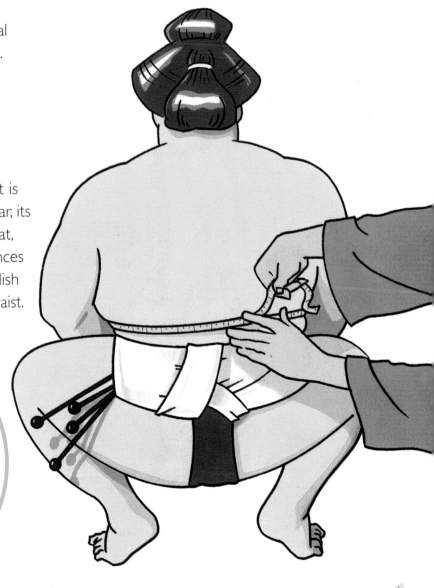

Did you know?
There are about 60,000 miles of tubes carrying blood around your body—long enough to stretch around the circumference of Earth an amazing 2½ times.

LONG AND SHORT UNITS

From earliest times, astronomers and scientists have struggled to measure lengths that would help them understand the universe.

The ancient Greeks were among the first people to study the distances of space. Some of the lengths used by scientists and astronomers today are too huge to imagine. Others are so short you cannot see them.

The first person known to have calculated Earth's circumference was a Greek, Eratosthenes, who lived in the third century B.C. Over the ages, other great astronomers, such as Copernicus, calculated the distances of space even more accurately. Scientists today have devised special units for extremely short and extremely long lengths. Modern space exploration relies on such units to make calculations that are as accurate as possible.

Length fact

A light year is a unit of measurement used to describe incredibly long distances in space. It is defined as the distance light waves travel through space in one year—about 5,900 billion miles.

Microscopic lengths

Scientists have expanded the metric system to include small and microscopic lengths. The units they use are shown below.

meter	1 m
decimeter	0.1 m
centimeter	0.01 m
millimeter	0.001 m
micrometer	0.000 001 m
nanometer	0.000 000 001 m
picometer	0.000 000 000 001 m
femtometer	0.000 000 000 000 001 m
attometer	0.000 000 000 000 000 001 m

Viruses and atoms

Can you imagine how small an attometer is, or what all those zeros after the decimal point really mean? The thickness of one page of this book is about 0.000125 meters, or 125 micrometers. Viruses, which give you illnesses such as the flu, are microscopically small—about 1 micrometer in length. But atoms are even tinier. They are less than 1 nanometer long.

Astronomic lengths

Scientists also use metric units to measure large and astronomic lengths.

meter	1 m
dekameter	10 m
hectometer	100 m
kilometer	1000 m
miriameter	10 000 m
megameter	1 000 000 m
gigameter	1 000 000 000 m
terameter	1 000 000 000 000 m

The longest unit of all

One of the brightest stars in the sky is called Antares. It is about 3,100,000,000,000,000 miles from Earth. This distance is equal to 4.9 million terameters, or about 520 light years. The parsec is one of the longest units used by scientists. It equals 3.26 light years. Even this is not long enough sometimes, so they use kiloparsecs (one thousand parsecs) and even megaparsecs (one million parsecs). These units help astronomers make incredibly complex calculations about distances in space.

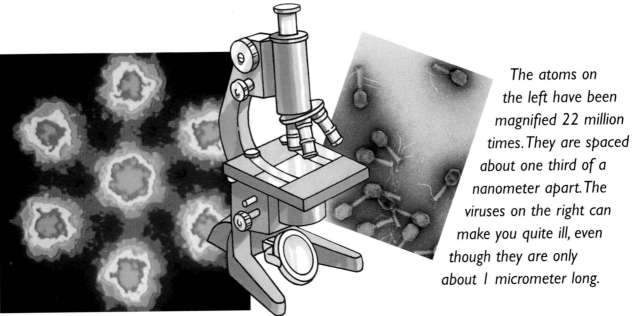

The atoms on the left have been magnified 22 million times. They are spaced about one third of a nanometer apart. The viruses on the right can make you quite ill, even though they are only about 1 micrometer long.

MEASURING WITH WAVES

Today scientists are able to measure difficult lengths by using radio, sound, and light waves. Systems such as radar and sonar allow them to measure with enormous accuracy.

Radar uses radio waves to measure distance. The system was primarily developed in the 1930s by an Englishman, Sir Robert Watson-Watt. Radio waves are sent out from a revolving dish. An echo is reflected back by any object that the waves hit, such as a plane or ship. The echo is picked up by the dish and sent to a computer that works out the distance and direction of the object.

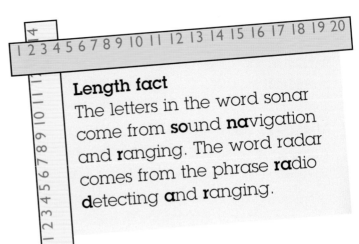

Length fact
The letters in the word sonar come from **so**und **na**vigation and **r**anging. The word radar comes from the phrase **ra**dio **d**etecting **a**nd **r**anging.

Sound waves

Sound can be used to measure distances underwater, such as the depth of the sea or the distance to an underwater object, such as a submarine or an iceberg. Sonar was first invented during World War I by American, British, and French scientists. Pulses of sound sent out by the ship hit any object in their path and bounce back to the ship like an echo. A special instrument measures the elapsed time and calculates how far the sound pulses have traveled. In the past, these instruments were called fathometers, because depth used to be measured in fathoms. Today, they are known as sonar devices or echo sounders.

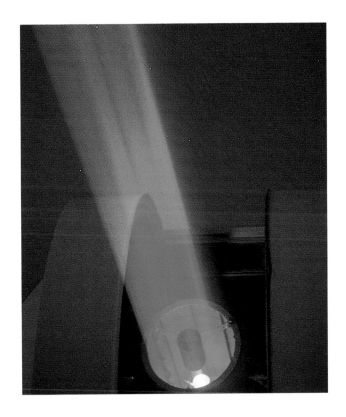

*The picture below
shows a radar screen
at an airport. Air
traffic controllers
use radar to check
the positions of all
the planes circling
around the airport.*

*A laser beam
is fired from
a telescope in
France (right).
The beam is
measuring the
distance from
Earth to the moon.*

Light waves

Scientists now use light waves to measure
both long and short distances with great
accuracy. Light waves are emitted from
a laser and are bounced off any object
in their path. A computer measures how
long the light waves take to return, which
allows it to calculate how far away the
object is. The first astronauts to the moon
placed a special mirror there called a
LIDAR (**li**ght ra**dar**). This device can
measure the huge distances from the
moon to Earth (on average 238,000 miles)
to an accuracy of a few inches. It is also
used to measure the distance between
any two places on our planet.

Standard meter

The original standard meter was a metal
bar, but since 1983, light waves have been
used to define the length of the standard
meter as accurately as possible.

MAPS AND SCALES

In order to use a map, it is important to understand map scale. Imagine how large a map would have to be if it was drawn life-size.

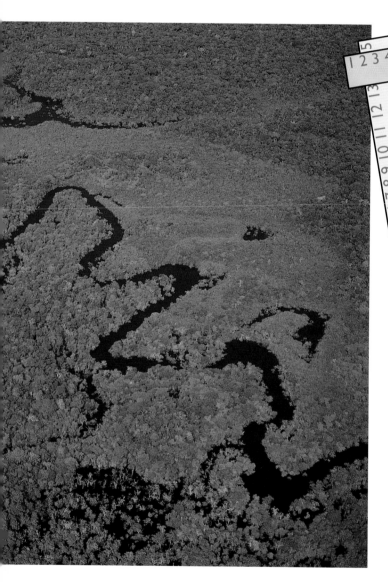

Length fact
Map makers scratch figures called bench marks on to walls and monuments. They show the height of the land at that point above sea level and are used to map contours accurately.

An aerial view of the Amazon River. The distances are small if you measure them on this page. In fact, the section of the river shown here measures several miles.

Looking at a map of a village, city, or country is like looking at a long-distance photograph taken from a great height. This is because when things are drawn to scale on a map, the actual distances are scaled down proportionally so that they will fit on a sheet of paper. Different maps have different scales, depending on how big the actual area is and how much detail is required. A large scale shows a small area in a lot of detail. A road map of a town or city might use a large scale to show each individual street. A small scale shows a greater area but less detail. This type of map would be useful if you wanted to plan a long road trip of hundreds of miles.

These maps show the same area using different scales. As the scale gets larger, you see less area but more detail, rather like zooming down from above.

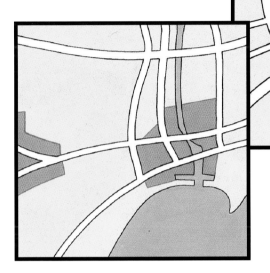

What does 1:60,000 mean?

To measure a real distance on a map, you need to know the exact scale of the map. A scale of 1:60,000 means that one unit of length on the map represents 60,000 of the same unit on the ground. So a road that is 1 inch long on the map is 60,000 inches long in reality. This equals almost 1 mile. In this way, drivers using a road map can make a rough estimate of the actual length of their journey.

Measuring with wheels

For making accurate measurements from a map, a small version of the trundle wheel can be used. You set the scale of the map on a dial and then push the wheel along the chosen route. The wheel converts the distance it travels in inches into the real journey distance in miles.

Contours

Contour lines on a map indicate mountains, hills and valleys. Each line is marked with a number—this is the height of the land above sea level in feet or meters. Everywhere along one line is the same height. Walkers and cyclists use such maps to work out how demanding their routes will be. Lines close together show steep land. Contours farther apart show a gentler slope.

When the contour lines on a map are close together like this, the land is very steep.

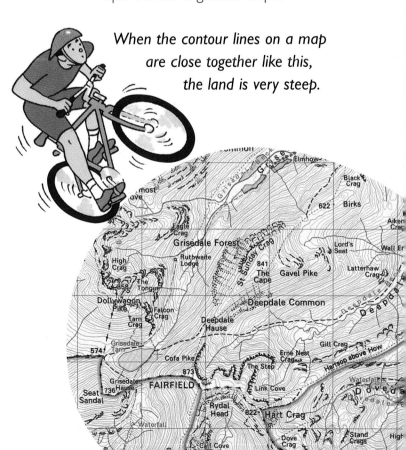

COMPARING LENGTHS

The United States uses both the U.S. customary and the metric systems of measurement. It is useful to compare both systems.

Very small lengths are measured in millimeters or fractions of an inch. A good working comparison is that 6 millimeters is about ¼ inch. A grain of rice is about this long. Short lengths are measured in centimeters or inches. One inch equals about 2.5 centimeters. The width of an adult's thumb is usually about 1 inch.

An average pen is about 6 inches or 15 centimeters long. You can measure more accurately using millimeters. This pen is 150 millimeters long.

how to change **centimeters to inches**	multiply by 0.39 36 cm = 36 x 0.39 in	= 14.04 in
how to change **inches to centimeters**	multiply by 2.54 9 in = 9 x 2.54 cm	= 22.86 cm
how to change **centimeters to feet**	multiply by 0.033 200 cm = 200 x 0.033 ft= 6.6 ft	
how to change **feet to centimeters**	multiply by 30.48 2 ft = 2 x 30.48 cm	= 60.96 cm

Meters, yards, and feet

Longer distances, such as the length of a room, can be measured in meters, feet, or yards. One meter is about the same as 3¼ feet, which is a little bit longer than 1 yard. The height of an inside door is usually 2 meters, or about 6½ feet.

Miles and kilometers

Really long lengths, such as the distance between two towns, are measured in miles or kilometers. A mile is longer than a kilometer. A useful comparison is that 5 miles is about 8 kilometers. At a steady pace, most people can walk about 3 miles or 5 kilometers in one hour.

A large bus like this is about 13 yards or 12 meters long. The distance the bus travels is measured in miles or kilometers.

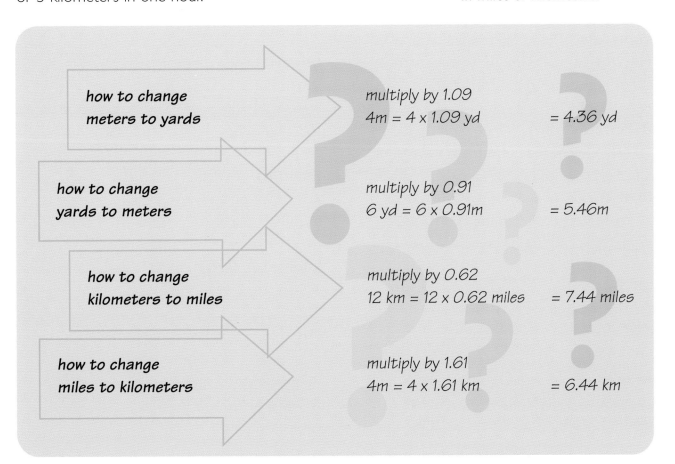

how to change meters to yards	multiply by 1.09 4m = 4 x 1.09 yd	= 4.36 yd
how to change yards to meters	multiply by 0.91 6 yd = 6 x 0.91m	= 5.46m
how to change kilometers to miles	multiply by 0.62 12 km = 12 x 0.62 miles	= 7.44 miles
how to change miles to kilometers	multiply by 1.61 4m = 4 x 1.61 km	= 6.44 km

LENGTHY WORDS

centimeter (cm) A metric unit of length. There are 100 centimeters in 1 meter.

chain An old English unit of 22 yards (about 20 meters), used for measuring land.

chang An ancient Chinese unit, equaling about 12 feet.

chih An ancient Chinese unit, equal to about 10 inches.

circumference The length around the edge of a circular object, such as Earth.

cubit An old unit, defined as the distance from the elbow to the tip of the middle finger, equal to about 20 inches.

decimeter (dm) A metric unit, equaling 10 centimeters. Ten decimeters equal 1 meter.

digit An old unit, defined as the width of the forefinger across the first joint. Sometimes called a **finger**.

ell The distance from elbow to elbow with fists touching the chest. The ell was used to measure cloth in the Middle Ages.

fathom A unit equal to 6 feet, used to measure the depth of water. It was defined as the distance between the fingertips with arms outstretched.

finger Another name for a **digit**.

foot (ft) An imperial unit. Originally the foot was simply the length from heel to toe. Today it is defined as a length of 12 inches (about 30 centimeters).

furlong An old unit of 220 yards (about 201 meters). There are 8 furlongs in a mile.

girth The distance around a person's waist.

hand The length across the palm with the fingers closed, including the thumb. As a standard unit it is 4 inches long.

imperial measures Common units of length used in Britain before metric lengths were introduced. They include miles, yards, feet, and inches.

inch (in) An imperial unit. The name comes from the Roman word *uncia*, meaning one twelfth. There are 12 inches in 1 foot.

kilometer (km) A metric unit. There are 1000 meters in a kilometer.

kus The Babylonian name for a cubit.

league An old unit, equal to 3 miles in Britain and the U.S. In France, a league was 4 kilometers long.

light year A unit used to measure huge distances in space. It is defined as the distance light travels through space in one year—about 5,900 billion miles.

meter (m) A metric length. There are 100 centimeters in 1 meter. One thousand meters equals 1 kilometer.

metric system A decimal system of measuring (based on the number ten). The main metric units are millimeters, centimeters, meters, and kilometers.

mile An imperial unit. The name comes from the Roman phrase *mille passus* – a thousand paces. Today 1 mile equals 1,760 yards.

millimeter (mm) A metric length. There are 10 millimeters in 1 centimeter.

nail An old unit commonly used for measuring cloth. It was the distance from the tip of the middle finger to the second joint, about 2¼ inches (about 5.5 centimeters).

nautical mile A unit for measuring distance at sea. In the UK it is just under 2,027 yards. An American nautical mile is 1 yard shorter.

pace The distance of one stride. The Roman pace was a double step of about 5 feet.

parsec A unit used by scientists and astronomers. It is equal to 3.26 light years.

perch Another name for a **rod**.

perimeter The distance measured around the edge of an object.

pole Another name for a **rod**.

rod An old measure of 5½ yards (about 5 meters) which was used to measure land. Sometimes called a **perch** or a **pole**.

royal foot A unit which matched the foot length of Emperor Charlemagne.

royal master cubit In ancient Egypt, this was the standard cubit length.

shusi An ancient unit equal to one thirtieth of a Babylonian cubit.

span The distance from the tip of the little finger to the tip of the thumb with fingers outstretched.

stadium An ancient Greek unit, equal to about 670 feet.

standard lengths Lengths that everyone agrees to use. Imperial, U.S. customary, and metric lengths are all standard units of length.

unit A standard measure of something which can represent length, weight, or volume.

U.S. customary units The system of lengths used in the United States, based on the British imperial system. They include miles, yards, feet, and inches.

yard (yd) An imperial unit, equal to 3 feet. There are 1,760 yards in a mile.

INDEX